IT'S TIME TO EAT A BELL PEPPER

It's Time to Eat a Bell Pepper

Walter the Educator

Silent King Books
A WhichHead Entertainment Imprint

Copyright © 2024 by Walter the Educator

All rights reserved. No part of this book may be reproduced in any manner whatsoever without written per- mission except in the case of brief quotations embodied in critical articles and reviews.

First Printing, 2024

Disclaimer

This book is a literary work; the story is not about specific persons, locations, situations, and/or circumstances unless mentioned in a historical context. Any resemblance to real persons, locations, situations, and/or circumstances is coincidental. This book is for entertainment and informational purposes only. The author and publisher offer this information without warranties expressed or implied. No matter the grounds, neither the author nor the publisher will be accountable for any losses, injuries, or other damages caused by the reader's use of this book. The use of this book acknowledges an understanding and acceptance of this disclaimer.

It's Time to Eat a Bell Pepper is a collectible early learning book by Walter the Educator suitable for all ages belonging to Walter the Educator's Time to Eat Book Series. Collect more books at WaltertheEducator.com

USE THE EXTRA SPACE TO TAKE NOTES AND DOCUMENT YOUR MEMORIES

BELL PEPPER

It's time to eat, hooray, hooray!

It's Time to Eat a

Bell

Pepper

A special snack comes out today!

Bell Pepper, Bell Pepper, green or red,

Yellow, orange—let's get fed!

We wash it clean, and take a look,

Round and shiny like a picture book.

It's crisp and fresh, so big and bright,

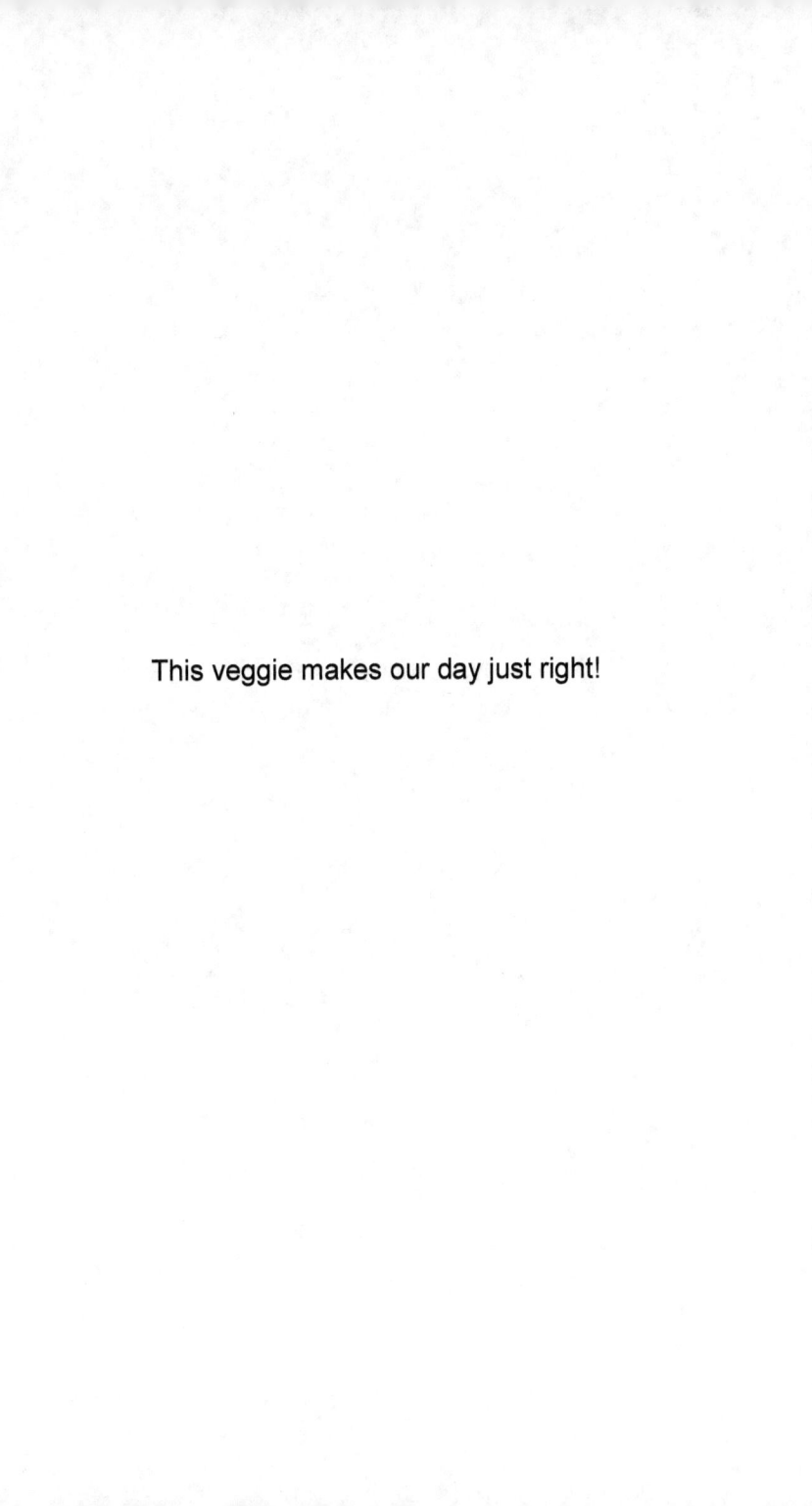

This veggie makes our day just right!

Crunchy, crunchy, take a bite,

Bell Pepper's flavor is a pure delight.

Sweet and mild, not spicy at all,

It's perfect to munch for big or small.

Cut in slices, strips, or rings,

Bell Pepper brings us lots of things!

In salads, soups, or on a plate,

Bell Pepper makes our snacks taste great!

It's Time to Eat a

Bell Pepper

With colors bold, it's fun to see,

Red, yellow, green—so rainbow-y!

We eat it raw or cooked up nice,

Bell Pepper adds some tasty spice.

In every meal, it loves to play,

At lunch or snack, it saves the day.

It gives us strength, helps us grow,

Bell Pepper's power is sure to show.

Let's dip it in some hummus, too,

Or munch it plain, just me and you!

With every bite, we crunch and smile,

Bell Pepper makes it all worthwhile.

So grab a slice, take a chew,

Bell Pepper fun for me and you!

It's Time to Eat a Bell Pepper

It's healthy, yummy, and so bright,

Bell Pepper time feels just right.

In every color, bold and sweet,

This veggie is a tasty treat!

So let's all share, no need to wait,

Bell Pepper's here—it's really great!

With every bite, we're full of cheer,

Bell Pepper time is finally here!

So munch away, enjoy each bite,

Bell Pepper fun from day to night!

ABOUT THE CREATOR

Walter the Educator is one of the pseudonyms for Walter Anderson. Formally educated in Chemistry, Business, and Education, he is an educator, an author, a diverse entrepreneur, and he is the son of a disabled war veteran. "Walter the Educator" shares his time between educating and creating. He holds interests and owns several creative projects that entertain, enlighten, enhance, and educate, hoping to inspire and motivate you. Follow, find new works, and stay up to date with Walter the Educator™

at WaltertheEducator.com

www.ingramcontent.com/pod-product-compliance
Lightning Source LLC
LaVergne TN
LVHW051925060526
838201LV00062B/4691